D1825646

Contents

Instructions

  means do this bit by yourself.

  means choose a partner and work together.

  means discuss this with the whole group.

Before you start...

Before using one of the tracks in this book, read the notes on
page 44 and the advice on specific tracks on pages 46 to 48.

What is God's

-LOAD-

Tony locked his bike to the stand, took his sports bag off the rack and headed towards the hall. As he turned the corner out of the bike shed something hit him in the stomach and he doubled up with pain and surprise.

'Oh, sorry mate!' said a voice, and several people laughed. As he stood up he was pushed sharply from behind. He fell against the side of the bike shed, and onto the ground. His bag flew out of his hand, sending several books spinning across the tarmac. More laughter.

Tony looked up to see a group of five older boys and a girl standing round him. One of them deliberately walked over his geography book, leaving a big footprint on the cover.

'Hey, get off!' shouted Tony. 'Get off my books.'

'Ooh!' sneered one of the boys. 'It talks!'

'It'd better not talk to any teachers though. That wouldn't be wise, would it lads? Not wise at all.'

They all laughed.

Tony picked himself up and gathered up his books. He had to pull one out from under the feet of some bloke who was standing on it. As he hurried off towards assembly he could hear them laughing behind his back.

'It's not fair,' he said to himself. 'How come I always get bullied? I wish I could....' He was about to say I wish I could thump them all, but he didn't *really* want that. On the other hand, why should they get away with it just 'cos they were big? It really isn't fair.

GROUP What you think Tony should do? Take a vote in the group to decide.

Take up body-building	.....
Tell a friendly teacher	.....
Put up with being bullied	.....
Fight back next time	.....
Forgive the people who attacked him	.....
Get some friends together and get his own back	.....
Something else	

Would your answer have been different if Tony had been a girl?

POWER SUPPLY

Six tracks about power for good and power for evil

Contributors :

Terry Dunnell
Andrew Graystone
Chris Powell

Scripture Union
130 City Road, London, EC1V 2NJ

Serendipity UK
48 Peterborough Road, London, SW6 3EB

In this series....

Going live — Living for God (ISBN 0 86201 668 1)

Tuned in — Knowing God (ISBN 0 86201 670 3)

Sounds like me — Am I OK? (ISBN 0 86201 665 7)

Making contact — Living with others (ISBN 0 86201 666 5)

System breakdown — What's gone wrong? (ISBN 0 86201 669 X)

Power supply — Power for good – power for evil (ISBN 0 86201 667 3)

© Serendipity UK 1990
First published 1990
ISBN 0 86201 667 3

British Library Cataloguing in Publication Data
Dunnell, Terry
   Power supply: power for good – power for evil.
   1. Young people. Christian life
   I. Title II. Graystone, Andrew III. Powell,
Chris IV. Series
   248.83

Printed by Ebenezer Baylis and Son Limited, The
Trinity Press, Worcester and London.

Acknowledgements
Cover design and artwork: Adept Design.
Internal artwork: Pauline Adams.
Series editor: Andrew Graystone.
Photograph by Gordon Gray.

action plan?

How do you think the bullies might have felt after they attacked Tony?

Mark an **X** somewhere on the line.

Happy ——————————————*Sad*

Why?

If you ruled the world for a day, what rules would you impose to make your kingdom a good place for everyone to live in? You can invent up to three rules.

Rule 1 ....

....

Rule 2 ....

....

Rule 3 ....

....

Now share your rules with the rest of the group and try to decide on just three rules from the whole group that would be good news for the people of your kingdom. Take a vote if necessary.

Rule 1 ....

....

Rule 2 ....

....

Rule 3 ....

....

Jesus said that God's plan (some times called God's kingdom) would be good news that would make people happy. What sort of things do people in this world *think* they need to make them happy? Put the top five in order of priority.

Money	.....	Good health	.....
Fame	.....	Nice house	.....
Good job	.....	Happy family	.....
Enough food	.....	Long life	.....
Good physique	.....	Brains	.....
Travel	.....	Quiet life	.....

Some people lack food, housing, money, jobs, clothes or friends. Make up some newspaper headlines that would be good news for some of those people.

THE DAILY M

STOP

Some people must have walked over 50 miles to see Jesus.

What does God have to say about his plan for us?

- Read the Bible passage.
- Mark any discoveries you make.
- Jot down any questions you are left with.
- Talk about your discoveries and questions with the group.....

Are there other sorts of 'poor' apart from not having any money?

PLAY

In this passage Jesus talks about the 'Kingdom of God' – the place and time where everything is done according to God's plan. It started when Jesus came and gets finished at the end of time.

When will these things happen?

WHEN Jesus had come down from the hill with the apostles, he stood on a level place with a large number of his disciples. A large crowd of people was there from all over Judea and from Jerusalem and from the coastal cities of Tyre and Sidon; they had come to hear him and to be healed of their diseases. Those who were troubled by evil spirits also came and were healed. All the people tried to touch him, for power was going out from him and healing them all.

Jesus looked at his disciples and said,

'Happy are you poor;
   the Kingdom of God is yours!
'Happy are you who are hungry now;
   you will be filled!
'Happy are you who weep now;
   you will laugh!
'Happy are you when people hate you, reject you, insult you, and say that you are evil, all because of the Son of Man! Be glad when that happens and dance for joy, because a great reward is kept for you in heaven. For their ances-

tors did the very same things to the prophets.

'But how terrible for you who are rich now;
  you have had your easy life!
'How terrible for you who are full now;
  you will go hungry!
'How terrible for you who laugh now;
  you will mourn and weep!
'How terrible when all people speak well of you; their ancestors said the very same things about the false prophets.

'But I tell you who hear me: Love your enemies, do good to those who hate you, bless those who curse you, and pray for those who ill-treat you. If anyone hits you on one cheek, let him hit the other one too; if someone takes your coat, let him have your shirt as well. Give to everyone who asks you for something, and when someone takes what is yours, do not ask for it back. Do for others just what you want them to do for you.'

Luke 6:17–31

What would people have thought when they heard Jesus say these things?

PLAY

Should we really do these things? Or was Jesus exaggerating to make a point?

What would happen if everybody in the world lived like this? What would happen if only some people did?

FAST FORWARD

TWOS According to God's plan, (his kingdom) which of these people are happy and which are sad? Put a ring round those who should be happy and put a cross through those who should be sad.

Wealthy • Hungry • Unemployed

Sad • Lonely • Powerful

Unpopular • Bullied • Popular

Bullies • Hurt • Poor

God's kingdom	This world's kingdom
eg People are important for who they are.	People are important for how wealthy they are.
....	....
....	....
....	....
....	....

TWOS Read the last paragraph of the Bible passage again. What is your response to the things Jesus says there?

You must be joking ❏
OK in Jesus' day but it wouldn't
    work now ❏
Let's be reasonable about this ❏
When do I start? ❏
It's only picture language ❏
Slap me someone! ❏

Other ....

GROUP Tony's experience is just one example of how the world's way of doing things (this world's kingdom) is different from God's plan. List some of the differences between the two kingdoms.

TWOS One of the signs of God's plan in action is that Jesus gave people good news. Another is that he healed people. Think about the places you know (school, work, home etc). What signs can you see of God's good news in action? Try to think of at least one each. (For example: 'at my school black kids get on with white kids'.)

....

....

SOLO Jesus didn't only heal people who were physically ill. Everybody needed Jesus' power to heal them. Are there any things in your life — such as bad memories, broken relationships or other hurts — that you would like Jesus to heal?

SOLO When Jesus prayed, 'Your kingdom come,' he was asking God to work out his plan for us. But he knew that God's plan was already well under way. So he lived according to God's plan by helping people, listening to people, accepting people, and setting people free wherever he was. What could you do to live out God's plan...

...in your home?
...in the place where you work?
...in this group?

WHAT WILL YOU DO?

Last month you lent some money to a friend to go on the youth club outing. She said she'd pay you back in a few days. But several weeks have passed and there is no sign of the money. Now she has come to you and asked if you'll lend her some money to buy a birthday present for her mum. What will you do?

‖PAUSE‖

GROUP Take some of this week's newspapers and look through them. Make a 'good news' wall-chart out of words, pictures and articles showing God's plan in action. Write on the chart: 'Your Kingdom has come.'

Now make a wall-chart headed: 'Your Kingdom will come.' Stick onto it words, pictures and articles about bad news places where God's plan is not yet worked out.

In silence Sit or kneel around the completed wall-charts. As you look at the items on the first chart, you could pray silently, 'Thank you, Lord, for this sign of your kingdom,' As you look at each item on the second chart, pray, 'Your kingdom come, Lord....'

TOUGH TALKING

If God's plan is good news, why do Christians still suffer?

Does God care about poor people more than rich people?

GOING FURTHER

If you want to think more about God's plan for the world, check out these Bible passages:

Jeremiah 31:23–34 –God's plan
Luke 4:16–22   –Jesus' mission
Matthew 10:5–23 –The disciples' mission

Can God

-LOAD-

It all started as a bit of a joke – just a way of passing a wet lunchtime. Then it became a habit. Pretty soon none of them dared miss a 'séance'.

Sharon would write out all the letters of the alphabet on slips of paper, and put them round the edge of a table. Then Nigel 'borrowed' a knife from the dining room and they started spinning it in the middle of the table to see what letters it would point to.

Lots of the time nothing happened. Then, one day, the knife pointed to the letters D–I–E. Suddenly the room felt really cold. Simon wanted to stop, but Nigel said they should see who it pointed to next. Everyone's heart was pounding as he spun the knife. When it stopped it was pointing at Sharon. She went white as a sheet. 'Look,'

said someone, 'it's pointing at her heart.'

The next day Sharon was off school. They all thought she'd died. She hadn't. But when Simon and Dawn went round to her house she was really shaken up. She'd been sick all day, and she was still white.

'Look, it's a load of nonsense,' Simon said as he walked home with Dawn. 'There's no demons and devils and stuff. That's all rubbish. We should never have started messing around with it in the first place.'

'How can you be so sure?' asked Dawn. 'I've seen this book about the occult in the library. It even tells you how to contact the spirit world. I think we should at least try it. It's the only way we'll find out if Sharon's going to be OK.'

So next day they all sat round in a circle....

eat the Devil?

Why...

...do you think they didn't dare miss a séance?
...do you think Simon wanted to stop?
...do you think Dawn wanted to go on?

Why do you think people like the group in the story get interested in contacting the spirit world? Tick the two most important factors or add your own.

Boredom ❏
Curiosity ❏
Desire for power ❏
Need to escape ❏
Wanting to know the future ❏
Wanting to control events ❏

....

....

What advice would you give to the group in the story?

What is your attitude to the occult?

It's very dangerous
    – don't get involved ❏
It's just a bit of fun
    – don't take it too seriously ❏

Other ....
....

The apostle Peter described the Devil as 'like a roaring lion, looking for someone to devour.'

Think of your own picture to describe the Devil, and draw or write it.

The power of the Devil can be real and terrible. But the power of Jesus is much greater. Tell each other about any times when you have seen the power of Jesus at work.....

....in the Bible.
....in your own experience.

How come Jesus was so relaxed?

STOP

What does God have to say about the power of Jesus?

- Read the Bible passages.
- Mark any discoveries you make.
- Jot down any questions you are left with.
- Talk about your discoveries and questions with the group.....

Would you have been frightened?

PLAY

These two incidents happened when the disciples hadn't known Jesus very long.

How do you think Jesus spoke to the waves and the evil spirit? What was his tone of voice?

JESUS got into a boat, and his disciples went with him. Suddenly a fierce storm hit the lake, and the boat was in danger of sinking. But Jesus was asleep. The disciples went to him and woke him up. 'Save us, Lord!' they said. 'We are about to die!'

'Why are you so frightened?' Jesus answered. 'How little faith you have!' Then he got up and ordered the winds and the waves to stop, and there was a great calm.

Everyone was amazed. 'What kind of man is this?' they said. 'Even the winds and the waves obey him!'

Matthew 8:23–27

Just then a man with an evil spirit in him came into the synagogue and screamed, 'What do you want with us, Jesus of Nazareth? Are you here to destroy us? I know who you are – you are God's holy messenger!'

Jesus ordered the spirit, 'Be quiet, and come out of the man!'

The evil spirit shook the man hard, gave a loud scream, and came out of him. The people were all so amazed that they started saying to one another, 'What is this? Is it some kind of new teaching? This man has authority to give orders to the evil spirits, and they obey him!'

Mark 1:23–27

What did the evil Spirit know about Jesus?

Why were the people so amazed? What's the best word to describe your reaction to these stories?

PLAY

What do these stories show us about the power of Jesus?

FAST FORWARD

TWOS Because Jesus calmed the storm on the lake, we can trust him to....(Tick one or more.)

Give us nice weather ❏
Calm the storms in our lives ❏
Be asleep when we need him ❏
Help us when we're afraid ❏
Talk to plants and make them grow ❏

Other ....

SOLO The storm in my life I would most like Jesus to calm is...

TWOS Because Jesus ordered the evil spirit to come out of the man we can trust him to....(Tick one or more.)

Do good magic tricks ❏
Help people who have got mixed
  up in the occult ❏
Make people keep quiet in church ❏
Clean out the evil things in our lives ❏
Take control of our lives if we let him ❏

Other ....

SOLO The area of my life that I would most like Jesus to take control of is...

GROUP Here's a danger list of some of the things the Devil can use to get a foothold in a person's life :

Tarot cards • fantasy games
ouija boards • palm reading • fortune telling,
horoscopes • drugs • satanic rock music,
mediums • black magic,
satanic science fiction books
and magazines.

What do all these things have in common?

GROUP Complete this sentence :

In this group we need Jesus' power to .....

....

....

Share your answers with the group.

WHAT WILL YOU DO?

Some friends invite you to their house to play a new game called 'Mystery and Magic'. It involves pretending to be a witch and casting spells on other players. They say it's not serious – just a bit of fun. And it's more fun if you play it in the dark. What will you do?

PAUSE

Football crowds often make up chants to cheer on their heroes or discourage the other side. Choose one of the verses below to give you inspiration, then make up a chant about the power of Jesus or the defeat of the Devil. How about this one:

Two, four, six, eight,
The Devil is the one we hate.
Three, five, seven, nine,
Jesus beats him every time!

Share your chants with the group and try out a few of them. Make as much noise as you can. Jesus' power is worth shouting about.

The Spirit who is in you is more powerful than the spirit in those who belong to the world *(1 John 4:4)*.

Resist the Devil, and he will run away from you. Come near to God, and he will come near to you *(James 4:7–8)*.

TOUGH TALKING

Some rock music talks about the Devil, and uses satanic symbols and words. Should Christians refuse to buy or listen to that sort of music?

Do evil spirits exist today? Do Christians have the power to cast them out as Jesus did? Are some illnesses really caused by evil spirits?

GOING FURTHER

If you want to think more about the power of the Devil and the greater power of Jesus, check out these Bible passages:

Deuteronomy 18:9–13
        –God's view on the occult
Ephesians 6:10–18
        –Armour for Christians
Revelation 20:7–10
        –The Devil defeated

Ideas for

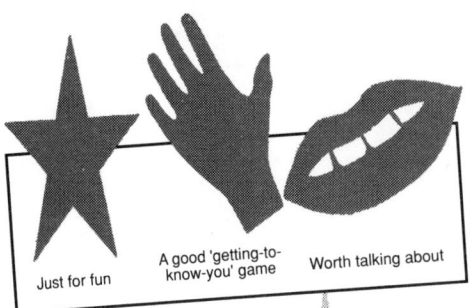

Just for fun   A good 'getting-to-know-you' game   Worth talking about

Indoor catch

This takes a bit of imagination! And it's a good way to get to know each other's names. Stand in a circle and ask everybody to say his or her name, just to make sure you know them all. One person then takes an imaginary tennis ball and throws it to another person, calling out their name. 'Catch, Nicky!' Nicky then throws it to someone else. 'Here you are, Debbie!' and so on. Keep throwing the invisible ball around the group making sure you use the catcher's name each time.

When you've been playing for a while, try exchanging your imaginary tennis ball for an imaginary beach ball, or an imaginary medicine ball, or even an imaginary jelly! In fact, let your imagination run wild!

The interview game

One person decides they need a job. That person leaves the room, and while they're gone the rest of the group chooses a job for which to interview them. For instance, you could interview them for the job of Blue Peter presenter, or Archbishop of Canterbury, or toothbrush tester.

When you've decided, call the person back in for an interview, but don't tell them what the job is. The group then starts asking questions. For a Blue Peter presenter you might ask questions like, 'Do you

like children?', 'Would you like to be famous?', 'Can you do creative things with a Fairy Liquid bottle?' Each question must give hints about the job, without giving the game away. The person being interviewed must answer the questions as if it were a real interview.

When you think the person knows what the job is you can offer it to them (without saying what it is!). The interviewee then replies, indicating what they think the answer is, eg 'Yes, I would like to be a Blue Peter presenter.'

Musical string

This game is a bit like musical chairs. Not much, but a bit! You need plenty of room to play it and a piece of string about fifteen centimetres long. Everyone walks round the outside of the room while the music plays, touching each wall as they pass it. Then when the music stops everyone tries to grab the piece of string from the middle. For each round, put just one piece of string in the middle. The person who succeeds in getting the piece of string sits out of future rounds, so everyone wins at least once. The publishers of this book accept no responsibility for any bones broken whilst playing this game!

Snuff-it

For this game you need three small bowls of water and three candles fixed securely in candle-holders or on saucers. You also need three pieces of string with a conker or cork threaded on one end and a peg attached to the other. Three volunteers at a time can play this game. Peg the string to the back of their clothes so that the conker

your group

or cork hangs thirty centimetres above the ground. Light the three candles. Without using their hands, the participants have to dip the conker or cork in the water, then run up to the candle and try to snuff it out using the wet conker or cork. The rest of you just stand back and watch. Try to give everyone a turn.

Rhinoceros and hippopotamus

You need two small objects; pens will do, or a couple of books, as long as they are different colours. Sit everyone in a circle. Player A starts with one object and passes it to player B, who is on his or her right, saying, 'This is a rhinoceros!' Player B takes it and asks, 'A what?' Player A replies, 'A rhinoceros!' Player B then passes the object to player C, the next person round the circle, saying, 'This is a rhinoceros!' Player C replies, 'A what?' Player B comes back to player A with, 'A what?' and player A replies, 'A rhinoceros!' Player B tells player C. Player C can then pass it to player D, and so on round the circle. Try to get a rhythm going as the object is passed round the room.

'But what about the other object?' I hear you cry! I was coming to that. When you've got the rhinoceros going round the circle, player A passes the other object to the person on his or her left, saying, 'This is a hippopotamus!' to which that player asks, 'A what?', – and so on.

Try it slowly first and you'll soon get the idea. But beware. When the two objects meet and pass (opposite player A) things suddenly get more complicated. Confused? Give it a go. You'll laugh a lot!

Four up

This is very simple, but absolutely fiendish! Everyone starts sitting down. Anyone in the group can stand up at any time, but you can only stay standing up for a maximum of five seconds before you sit down again. After that you can get straight up again if you wish. The aim is to have exactly four people standing up at all times. Sounds easy? Try it!

A load of rubbish!

It's amazing how much rubbish human beings create. But it's equally amazing how much fun you can have with it.

SCRAPARAMA Collect together clean bits of household rubbish such as toilet rolls, plastic bottles, paint tins, cardboard boxes.... Divide the rubbish into roughly equal piles and give one to each team. Then give everyone half an hour to create a monster (or it could be a machine to solve one of the world's problems!) Provide a central pool of equipment such as scissors, paste, rubber bands, paint. At the end take time to admire each other's creations.

GREAT EGG RACE This is a variation on Scraparama. Provide the same piles of scrap and equipment. But this time the challenge is to build a machine that will carry a raw egg as far as possible across the room under its own propulsion. When the time's up have a 'Great Egg Race'. Eggs that get scrambled are disqualified!

Money and things

LOAD

Talk about mean!

Every Saturday Dawn works in the kitchens at The Fox and Dogs heaving dirty plates in and out of the washer till she's got arms like a sumo wrestler.

It's not that she's into washing up in a big way. The last time she did it at home was before Christmas, and that was to pay off a debt. No, Dawn is strictly in it for the money.

She's not poor either. What with her pocket money and money from her Gran each week and her earnings from the Fox and Dogs she must get twice as much as the rest of us. More even. Poor Marcus doesn't have a cent since his dad left. But however much she's got it never seems to be enough for Dawn. She's always wanting something else.....clothes, albums, electrical stuff. Her bedroom's like an Argos catalogue. It's always the latest....always the best....and she doesn't mind telling you so.

The stupid thing is she's always the one who's forgotten her sub for the club on Friday night. So some mug has to pay her in, and then she'll sponge off someone else for a drink at half time.

On Saturday night you'll find her flashing round the rink in her fancy gear. (She's got her own skates of course.) She'll never buy you a drink..... not even give you a fag. And last week when Marcus was 10p short for the bus home, do you know what she did? She made him walk.

Talk about mean!

TWOS What is your attitude to Dawn? (Tick one or more, or add your own.)

She's earnt it – good luck to her ❏
I wish I had her money ❏
I feel sorry for her ❏
I wouldn't like to know her ❏
She sounds like a good laugh ❏
Where did you say she lives? ❏

Other...

TWOS Why do you think money is so important to Dawn?

who's in charge?

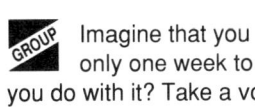 Imagine that you have £10,000 but only one week to live. What would you do with it? Take a vote in the group.

Throw a wild party for all your friends   .....
Take a trip round the world   .....
Buy a Porsche and do 120 mph
     up the motorway   .....
Set up a home for stray dogs   .....
Give all the money to a Third
     World charity   .....
Pay for a memorial statue of yourself   .....
Make large gifts to your friends   .....
Do nothing. Carry on as normal   .....

 Think back to the last time you earned any money. If you have a regular job think back to your last week's pay.

How did you earn it?

....

How much did you earn?

£..
What did you do with it?

....

Do you think you used the money well?

....

Tell the rest of the group about it, if you want to.

 How we spend our money is a good test of what our priorities are. How do you spend your money? Put a 1 by the item you spend most money on, a 2 by the item you spend the second most on, and so on.

 Clothes   .....

 Savings   .....

 Entertainment / outings   .....

 Food and drink   .....

 Presents   .....

 'Housekeeping'   .....

 Hobbies   .....

 Gifts to charities / church   .....

Other ....

 Compare your answers with the others in the group. What are the top priorities for your group?

1...

2...

3...

How do you feel about this?

Was Jesus criticising people for having possessions?

■STOP■

What does God have to say about money and possessions?

- ■ Read the Bible passages.
- ■ Mark any discoveries you make.
- ■ Jot down any questions you are left with.
- ■ Talk about your discoveries and questions with the group.....

What was the farmer's main aim in life?

PLAY▶

Jesus said to the crowd....

What was the farmer's big mistake?

'WATCH out and guard yourselves from every kind of greed; because a person's true life is not made up of the things he owns, no matter how rich he may be.'

Then Jesus told them this parable: 'There was once a rich man who had land which bore good crops. He began to think to himself, "I haven't anywhere to keep all my crops. What can I do? This is what I will do," he told himself; "I will tear down my barns and build bigger ones, where I will store my corn and all my other goods. Then I will say to myself, Lucky man! You have all the good things you need for many years. Take life easy, eat, drink and enjoy yourself!" But God said to him, "You fool! This very night you will have to give up your life; then who will get all these things you have kept for yourself?"'

What does it mean to be 'rich in God's sight'?

PLAY

And Jesus concluded, 'This is how it is with those who pile up riches for themselves but are not rich in God's sight.'

Luke 12:15–21

On another occasion, Jesus said....

'**D**o not start worrying "Where will my food come from? or my drink? or my clothes?" (These are the things the pagans are always concerned about.) Your Father in heaven knows that you need all these things. Instead, be concerned above everything else with the Kingdom of God and with what he requires of you, and he will provide you with all these other things.'

Matthew 6:31–33

Why are the pagans always concerned about these things? Why do Christians not need to be?

pagans, n. pl. An old-fashioned word for people who don't worship the real God.

What does God require of us?

FASE FORWARD

 Unjumble these letters and use them to fill the gaps in both these sentences :

L R E E N T A

The things that we need for this life _ _ _

_ _ _ _ to us by God. Only our relationship

with him is _ _ _ _ _ _ _.

SOLO How much do you care about....

(a) What you eat
1 2 3 4 5 6 7 8 9 10

(b) What you drink
1 2 3 4 5 6 7 8 9 10

(c) What you wear
1 2 3 4 5 6 7 8 9 10

(d) God's kingdom
1 2 3 4 5 6 7 8 9 10

(e) What God requires
1 2 3 4 5 6 7 8 9 10

Ring one number on each line. (1 = it's my number one priority, 10 = never think about it.)

TWOS According to the Bible passages you have just read, why do we not need to worry about items a, b and c?

....

....

What will happen if we concentrate our concern on items d and e?

....

....

SOLO What two items or activities would you find hardest to shift to a lower priority in life?

Special people ❏
Buying the latest clothes ❏
My record/tape/CD collection ❏
My relationship with Jesus ❏
Watching TV ❏
My favourite hobby ❏
Talking on the telephone ❏
Belonging to this group ❏
My school work/job prospects ❏
Making money ❏

Other ....

GROUP 'Be concerned above everything else with the Kingdom of God and with what he requires.' As a group, how could we help each other to do what he requires.....

...with our possessions?
....with our money?
....with our time?

TWOS If this group had £100 to put to a good use, what do you think God would want you to do with it?

GROUP Which idea do you like best? How could you go about getting £100 to put the idea into practice?

WHAT WILL YOU DO?

All your friends are planning a binge to celebrate the end of exams. They're going out for a meal, on to a concert and rounding the evening off at an expensive night club with a coach to bring them home.

You are invited, but you know it will mean you don't have any cash left for the rest of the month. What will you do?

GOING FURTHER

If you want to think more about money and possessions check out these Bible passages:

1 Timothy 6:6–11 –True riches

Matthew 19:16–30–Follow Jesus, not money

Luke 19:11–27 –Use what God gives

TOUGH TALKING

A rich young man asked Jesus how he could get to heaven. Jesus told him to sell everything he had and give it to the poor (Matthew 19:16–22). He also told his disciples to do the same thing (Luke 12:32–34). Should we take this instruction literally? If not, what does it mean?

Some people say that if you dedicate your life to God, you can expect him to make you financially successful. Can you think of any parts of the Bible that support or challenge this view?

Power and

LOAD

'Hey! Gazzer! What happened in physics? We could hear the shouting next door.'

'Angie Stephens, that's what happened. Jenkins sent her to the head.'

'What for?'

'When Jenkins came in someone had written "Black bastards" on the board, and Jenkins gets Sanjit out and starts laying into him asking him who did it and what he'd done to provoke them.

'Then Angie gets up and tells him to lay off Sanjit. So Jenkins says "Sit down!" and Angie says, "I won't 'cos you're always giving Sanjit hassle just because he's black, like you do all us black kids."

'So he says, "Listen here young lady!" and she says, "My name is Angie, and stop patronising me." Then he says, "I'm not being spoken to like that, even by an over-emotional girl!"

'Angie's really steaming now and she says, "Stop putting me down just 'cos I'm a woman. You're always making the girls look stupid. It's time you started treating everyone in your class like people." So Jenkins looks around the class and says, "I don't see anyone else complaining of unfair treatment. Anyone want to join Miss Stephens outside the head's office, hmm?" And he sent her out.'

'But what about the rest of you? Didn't you stick up for her?'

'Against a teacher? You must be joking.'

GROUP How do you think Sanjit felt through all this? Think of any words that might describe his feelings, and write them here.

TWOS Imagine the conversation between Angie and the headteacher. Assume that Angie is right in saying that Mr Jenkins treats people differently depending on whether they are black or white. Fill in Angie's answers to the head's questions. Or if you like you could act out the conversation with your partner.

'Well Angie, why are you here?'

prejudice: who wins?

 GROUP What sort of people are sometimes treated unfairly or subject to prejudice in our society? Think of as many as you can and note them down here.

eg Black people.

 TWOS This symbol means 'No nuclear weapons here'.

This symbol means 'No smoking'.

Think of a symbol to say 'No prejudice here'.

 TWOS What do you think the head teacher should do or say...

...to Angie?
...to Sanjit?
...to Mr Jenkins?

 SOLO Have you ever seen someone being treated unfairly like Sanjit was? What happened? How did you feel?

Have you ever treated someone unfairly in that way?

If you answered 'yes' to either of the above questions, tell the group anything that you have learnt from your experience.

STOP

What does God have to say about prejudice?

- ■ Read the Bible passage.
- ■ Mark any discoveries you make.
- ■ Jot down any questions you are left with.
- ■ Talk about your discoveries and questions with the group.....

How honest do you think the Pharisee was?

PLAY

Jesus told this parable to people who were sure of their own goodness and despised everybody else.

Do you think the Pharisee knew the tax collector personally?

'ONCE there were two men who went up to the Temple to pray: one was a Pharisee, the other a tax collector.

'The Pharisee stood apart by himself and prayed, "I thank you, God, that I am not greedy, dishonest, or an adulterer, like everybody else. I thank you that I am not like that tax collector over there. I fast two days a week, and I give you a tenth of all my income."

Why did the Pharisee think God would be pleased with him?

Why wouldn't the tax collector look up?

Pharisee, n. A member of a very strict Jewish group.

'But the tax collector stood at a distance and would not even raise his face to heaven, but beat on his breast and said, "God, have pity on me, a sinner!" I tell you,' said Jesus, 'the tax collector, and not the Pharisee, was in the right with God when he went home. For everyone who makes himself great will be humbled, and everyone who humbles himself will be made great.'

Luke 18:10–14

Tax collectors were hated because they lived by fiddling people's tax bills. This man was probably a Jew who worked for the Roman authorities.

Was the tax collector being too hard on himself?

PLAY

What had the tax collector got right and the Pharisee got wrong?

FASE FORWARD

TWOS Complete this sentence:

The Pharisee and the tax collector were both...

but only the tax collector knew....................

....

TWOS Draw lines connecting the words on the left with the bits on the right which you think fit best.

God was pleased with the tax collector because

■ he was honest about his faults
■ he looked down on other people
■ he was very religious
■ he asked for God's help
■ he did not recognise his own needs

God was not pleased with the Pharisee because

TWOS What do you think would help the Pharisee to overcome his prejudice?

Avoiding tax collectors in future ☐
Being more humble ☐
Getting to know some tax collectors ☐
Praying a bit harder ☐
Understanding what really pleases God ☐

Other ....

SOLO How much of the Pharisee and how much of the tax collector do you see in your own life? Put a percentage for each. (The two must add up to 100%)

I see myself as ....% Pharisee

and ....% tax collector.

SOLO The person or group of people I find most difficult to love is....

....
To start loving this person or group I need

to...

....

GROUP Every person in your group is the best at something....everyone has something unique to contribute to the group. On the left hand side, list the names of everyone in your group. Then beside each name write something unique and special they bring to the group.

The special thing about...   ...is....

eg Dave   his cheerfulness

....

....

....

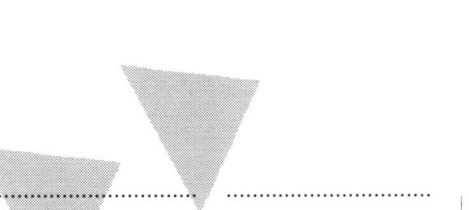

||PAUSE||

....

....

....

WHAT WILL YOU DO?

You are going to a rather posh disco with a group of friends, one of whom is black. The doorman says that your black friend can't come in 'because he's not properly dressed'. The others want to go in anyway. What will you do?

TOUGH TALKING

Why do groups of people who are unfairly treated sometimes resort to violence to get their way? Are they right to do this?

Are Christians ever treated unfairly because of their faith? Has this ever happened to you?

GOING FURTHER

If you want to think more about prejudice and how to avoid it, check out these Bible passages:

Galatians 3:26–29 –All one in Christ Jesus

Luke 10:25–37 –A lesson from an outsider

1 Samuel 16:1–13 –God looks at the heart

GROUP Read together Matthew 25:31–46 (or ask someone to read it while the rest of you close your eyes and listen.) In this passage Jesus says that whatever we do to welcome or reject 'outsiders', we are really doing to him.

Close your eyes. Imagine that Jesus came to your group. What would you do to welcome him? Imagine he was hungry when he arrived. What would you do for him? Have someone read out these statements while the rest of you keep their eyes closed. After each statement one or more people say what they will do for Jesus.

eg Reader: Jesus is hungry
Response: *I'll make him a sandwich*

Now read the following and say what you will do about them. You could make up your own examples too.

Jesus is in a wheelchair.
Jesus is lonely.
Jesus is cold – he hasn't got a coat.
Jesus is teased at school because he's black.
Jesus is tired.
Jesus is sad.

Ask Jesus to give you the opportunity to serve him this week by caring for an 'outsider'.

MANY people say that competition is inevitable. Others say that God intended us to live in co-operation not competition – working together, not trying to beat everyone else. What do you think? Chris Powell says, when you co-operate instead of competing, ...

Everyone's a winner

First of all Chris, what do you mean by competition?

People compete in many different ways. Some are obvious – playing tennis or Monopoly, or even trying to get a boy-friend or girl-friend who someone else fancies. Other ways of competing are less obvious – our clothes and hairstyles can be competitive if we're trying to look trendier or more attractive than other people. Even talking can be competitive when one person wants their opinion heard more than someone else's.

So you're saying it's pretty widespread.

Competition affects just about every part of life all over the world. It affects the prices in the shops, the wages people are paid, the way rich countries treat poor countries, the way people treat the rain forests – and it affects the way people are valued.

So what's the problem?

The problem is, wherever there is comp-etition – of whatever sort – there is a winner and a loser. And I think that both can be damaged by the experience. If you're a winner you can start to value people on the basis of how well they do things rather than who they are. If you're a loser you can end up with a sense of failure.

Some people might say that competition encourages people to try harder and achieve more.

That's not true for people who continually fail. It only discourages them. Eventually they may give up altogether.

Aren't all games competitive?

Not necessarily. Take *Four up* or *Indoor catch* from the *Meeting points* pages. There are no winners or losers in those games but they're loads of fun.

What about team sports. Don't they develop co-operation and team-work?

Maybe they do. But only with the purpose of beating others. Co-operation can be so much more fun than competition because everyone can participate and no one ends up feeling put down or useless or a loser.

The young people we asked said...

A WINNER IS...
HAPPY SKILLED PROUD
A CHEAT ADMIRED pushy
NUMBER ONE "THE BEST"
Lucky

A LOSER IS...
RUBBISH unfortunate
everyone is UNABLE
USELESS THICK

IS your group competitive? Could it be more co-operative?

WHAT about the games and sports you play; can everyone really join in?

WHAT about the way you talk and discuss things; do some people always compete to make their voice heard?

WHAT about other things; is there pressure to dress better than each other, or to have more possessions than each other, or to do more daring things than each other?

WHAT DO YOU THINK ?

WE asked a group of young people in Coventry for their thoughts about winners and losers. This is what they said...

When I win I feel...
'Really pleased with myself.'
'Pleased if it meant effort on my part.'
'Proud, complete.'

When I lose I feel...
'Lousy, fed-up.'
'OK unless I've been wanting to win too badly.'
'Mad at myself.'

Should Christians be co-operative instead of competitive?
'You have to become united not competitive.'
'In life you have to be competitive.'
'As a Christian if you settle for not being competitive you won't get anywhere; no job, no money, nothing.'
'We're competing against evil.'

WHY NOT?

◆ ....use these pages to think about competition in your group.

◆ ....check out some of the questions in the box. Talk about them together.

◆ ....play some of the games in the *Meeting points* section. Notice whether they're competitive or co-operative.

Should we always

LOAD

Jane works Saturdays in the posh bread shop on Front Street. At least, she works there *now*. She might not work there much longer. You see she's thinking of leaving. That's if she doesn't get fired first.

She came home last Saturday after work and she was nearly in tears. So we all got round and asked her what was wrong. It turns out the bread shop, which everyone thinks is the best in town, is actually ripping off its customers left, right and centre.

'What am I supposed to do?' Jane asked us. 'The manager takes last week's bread out of the freezer and puts a sign on it saying "Fresh this morning." When the customers ask me if the cakes are home-made he wants me to say, "yes". It's a lie.

They come in a lorry from the factory. I told him I didn't want to lie to the customers, but he just said, "If you don't like it, you don't have to work here." He'd sell his own granny if he could get a good price for her. What am I supposed to do? It's not fair to the customers. But he *is* my boss.'

'Quite agree,' said Terry. 'Christians are supposed to do what they're told aren't they?'

'Rubbish!' said Angela. 'You must tell the customers the truth, even if he gives you the sack for it.'

'No way, man,' said Hugh. 'Just grit your teeth and do as you're told. You can't give up a good job just for the sake of a few white lies.'

do as we're told?

TWOS What do you think would happen if Jane refused to lie to the customers? Choose the answer you think is most likely, or think of your own.

The boss would respect her for
  her honesty ❑
She would get the sack ❑
The manager would stop lying to his
  customers ❑
The customers would treat her
  like a hero ❑
The manager would become a Christian ❑

Other ....

GROUP What advice would you give to Jane? See if you can agree on what you think she should do.

TWOS Each of these people has to make or enforce rules. Finish the sentences that describe the purpose of their job.

eg A *headteacher* makes school rules so that *the school can run smoothly.*

A *cricket umpire* keeps the laws of cricket so that ...

....

A *member of parliament* makes laws so that ...

....

A *parent* makes family rules so that ...

....

A *policeman* enforces the law so that ...

....

GROUP Make a list of all the people who have some sort of authority in your life, eg parents, teachers.

....

....

....

....

SOLO Think of one time when you have gone against what someone in authority told you to do. Why did you do it? (Tick one or more.)

I don't like being told what to do ❑
What they were telling me to do went
  against what God would want ❑
It was an accident – I didn't know I was
  doing anything wrong ❑
I was sure I wouldn't get caught ❑
I thought I had a better idea ❑
I just wanted to do it ❑

Other ....

Why didn't Jesus give a straight Yes or No to this question?

STOP

What does God have to say about people in authority?

- Think about the Bible passages.
- Mark any discoveries you make.
- Jot down any questions you are left with.
- Talk about your discoveries and questions with the group.....

They meant the Jewish laws

PLAY

In Jesus' time the Romans made the Jews pay a heavy and unpopular poll tax. Jesus' enemies tried to use it to get him into trouble.

Why do you think Jesus said this? What did he mean?

SOME Pharisees and some members of Herod's party were sent to Jesus to trap him with questions. They came to him and said, 'Teacher, we know that you tell the truth, without worrying about what people think. You pay no attention to a man's status, but teach the truth about God's will for man. Tell us, is it against our Law to pay taxes to the Roman Emperor? Should we pay them or not?'

But Jesus saw through their trick and answered, 'Why are you trying to trap me? Bring a silver coin, and let me see it.'

They brought him one, and he asked, 'Whose face and name are these?'

'The Emperor's,' they answered.

So Jesus said, 'Well, then, pay the Emperor what belongs to the Emperor, and pay God what belongs to God.'

And they were amazed at Jesus.

Mark 12:13–17

PETER and John were still speaking to the people when some priests, the officer in charge of the temple guards, and some Sadducees arrived. They were annoyed because the two apostles were teaching the people that Jesus had risen from death, which proved that the dead will rise to life. So they arrested them and put them in jail until the next day.....

They called them back in and told them that on no condition were they to speak or to teach in the name of Jesus. But Peter and John answered them, 'You yourselves judge what is right in God's sight – to obey you or to obey God. For we cannot stop speaking of what we ourselves have seen and heard.'

Acts 4:1–3, 18–20

In the year after Jesus died, Peter and John were arrested and ordered to stop speaking about him. They had to decide whether it was right to do as they were told or disobey the authorities.

The Sadducees did not believe in life after death.

How do you think Peter and John felt when they were arrested?

Why did they decide to disobey the authorities?

Did Jesus say they should pay the tax or not?

PLAY

FAST FORWARD

Here are some statements about how we relate to people in authority. According to the Bible passages you have just read, which of these statements are true and which are false?

	True	False
We should only obey the authorities if we feel like it	.....	.....
God gives us leaders to guide and protect us	.....	.....
Christians should always do as they're told	.....	.....
We should obey the authorities – but we should put God first	.....	.....

The Bible as a whole says we should normally do what people in authority tell us to. Why do you think this might be so?

Because they are bigger and
stronger than us ❏
Because they have the benefit of
experience ❏
Because they are doing a job God has
given them ❏
Because we might be in authority
one day ❏
Because they are trying to protect
us from harm ❏
Because we want a quiet life ❏

Other ....

Is it ever right *not* to do as you're told?

Yes ❏   No ❏

Can you think of a time when it might be right not to obey someone in authority? Share your ideas with the group.

Which member of your group would you choose for each of the following responsibilities? Find a job for every member of the group. Think of some more job titles if you need to.

Captain of the first mission to Mars

....
Scriptwriter for a new TV comedy show

....
Coach to the Olympic athletics team

....
Ambassador to the United Nations

....
Chief cook to the royal family

....
Young people's representative on the church council or diaconate

....

Now tell everyone what job you have chosen for them!

WHAT WILL YOU DO?

You belong to a Christian Union group that meets in your school at lunchtime. The headteacher decides to ban the group from advertising or holding meetings anywhere in the school buildings. What will you do?

TOUGH TALKING

Should a Christian be a member of a political party? How should a Christian decide which party to vote for?

When this country was at war, many Christians joined the armed forces and fought for their country, but some refused. Were they right to do so? What would you do if there was a war and all young people were called up to fight?

PAUSE

Paul wrote to Timothy

TWOS I urge, then, first of all, that requests, prayers, intercession and thanksgiving be made for everyone – for kings and all those in authority, that we may live peaceful and quiet lives in all godliness and holiness *(1 Timothy 2:1, 2 NIV)*.

Fill in the gap in this prayer, using just a few words. Then pray it in the group or in your pair.

Thank you Lord for *our parents,* who you have given us. We pray that you will help them ....
....

Now use the same prayer outline to make up simple prayers for....

....your teachers or your boss
....the local police
....your member of parliament or local councillor
....your church leader
....and anyone else in authority who needs your prayers.

GOING FURTHER

If you want to think more about people in authority, check out these Bible passages:

Romans 13:1–7 – Obey the authorities, says Paul

1 Peter 2:13–17 – Freedom and respect

How should Christ

LOAD–

The bus was packed as usual, but Mark was in his own little world. It was decision time. The phone call had to be made today.

'Morning, misery!' said Rachel, digging him in the ribs. 'Has your dad cut your pocket money or did the cat die?'

'Hi, Rachel', said Mark, jolting awake. 'The answer's, "No, no, and yes, I'm hassled."'

'I'm listening', said Rachel.

'I've got this decision to make by tonight but I can't make up my mind. Should I take up my place at college or should I spend a year on the voluntary service scheme? I really....'

Rachel interrupted. 'You're not serious are you? Spend a year working your socks off in some grimy industrial town when you could be at college? No choice! I know what I would do!'

'It's not that simple and it's not that bad. I'd really like to do the scheme. It'd be different. And anyway, I think God wants me to do it. But Dad's not too keen,' replied Mark as they piled off the bus and walked up the school drive

'That's the trouble with you, Mark – you take God too seriously. You only live once and you've got to get qualified. College is going to be brilliant. How can you live for a year on pocket money? Anyway, the decision is yours. I know what I'd do.'

ans handle power?

 What do you think Mark would find hardest? (Choose three and put them in order.)

Postponing going to college for a year ..... \
Living on pocket money for a year ..... \
Going against his dad's advice ..... \
Caring for other people ..... \
Living in a strange town ..... \
Leaving his family ..... \
Leaving his friends and his church ..... \
Going to college .....

Other ....

 Do you agree or disagree with Rachel's advice? Why?

 Have you ever felt that God was asking you to do something hard that involved putting someone else first? What did you do? What happened? Share some of your stories with the group.

Fill in the gaps in these sentences using the words 'always' 'sometimes' or 'never'.

God .... asks us to put other people first.

Serving other people is .... easy.

 Jesus said that the greatest commandments were, 'Love the Lord your God with all your heart, with all your soul, and with all your mind,' and 'Love your neighbour as you love yourself.' Which is the most difficult for you? (Tick one.)

To love God with all my heart \
(hopes and ambitions) ❑ \
To love God with all my soul \
(feelings and emotions) ❑ \
To love God with all my mind \
(beliefs and ideas) ❑ \
To love my neighbour \
(friends, family and others) ❑ \
To love myself ❑

 If Jesus had come to earth in the twentieth century, what job do you think he would have taken? Take a vote in the group.

Housewife ..... Vicar ..... \
Lorry driver ..... \
Tramp ..... \
Nurse ..... Rock star .....

STOP

What does God have to say about how we should treat each other?

- Read the Bible passage.
- Mark any discoveries you make.
- Jot down any questions you are left with.
- Talk about your discoveries and questions with the group....

Does God sometimes take the bad things people do and use them for good purposes? Does anyone in the group have any examples?

What sort of power did Jesus have?

PLAY

In Jesus' time when you went into a house the lowest servant washed everyone's hot sticky feet. At supper a few days before he died Jesus did a shocking thing. He washed his disciples' feet.

JESUS and his disciples were at supper. The Devil had already put into the heart of Judas, the son of Simon Iscariot the thought of betraying Jesus. Jesus knew that the Father had given him complete power; he knew that he had come from God and was going to God. So he rose from the table, took off his outer garment, and tied a towel round his waist. Then he poured some water into a basin and began to wash the disciples' feet and dry them with the towel round his waist. H

Why didn't one of the disciples wash everyone's feet?

What would the disciples have been thinking?

PLAY!

came to Simon Peter, who said to him, 'Are you going to wash my feet, Lord?'.....

After Jesus had washed their feet, he put his outer garment back on and returned to his place at the table. 'Do you understand what I have just done to you?' he asked. 'You call me Teacher and Lord, and it is right that you do so, because that is what I am. I, your Lord and Teacher, have just washed your feet. You, then, should wash one another's feet.'

John 13:2–6, 12–14

If you had been one of the disciples and Jesus had washed your feet, how would you have felt? What would you have said?

What does this instruction mean? Whose 'feet' should we 'wash', and how?

FAST FORWARD

Think of a good excuse for....

TWOS ....taking the last biscuit in the packet

....

....pushing to the front of the bus queue

....

....not caring about needy people in the Third World

....

SOLO Tick any of these answers that apply, or make up your own....

The most difficult thing for me about serving other people is....

....people don't seem to need any help ❏
....I have nothing to give ❏
....people don't admit they need anything ❏
....I'm shy and I don't like to intrude ❏
....I'm too proud ❏

Other ....

GROUP Jesus said that he did not come to be served but to serve. What would happen if the following people took the same attitude?

Politicians and world leaders
Members of your church
Members of this group

TWOS Which of these do you think Jesus would say was the most important thing for his followers to be concerned about? Mark it with a tick. Which do you think he would say was the least important? Mark it with a cross.

Knowing the Bible ❏
Being active in the church ❏
Providing housing for the homeless ❏
Working for justice ❏
Developing your own potential ❏
Praising and worshipping God ❏
Telling people about Jesus ❏
Being friendly and caring for the lonely ❏

SOLO Think of two people you look up to:

....

....

Now think of two people who look up to you:

....

....

In what ways could you be a 'servant' to these people? In what ways could you 'wash their feet'?

WHAT WILL YOU DO?

The other members of the group are going out to a concert and they have invited you. Without knowing about the concert, your parents ask you if you will stay in and look after your little brother so they can have a night out. What will you do?

TOUGH TALKING

'God helps those who help themselves.' Do you agree?

GOING FURTHER

If you want to think more about being a 'servant', check out these Bible passages:

Mark 10:35–45 – Who is the greatest?

Ezekiel 34:1–10– A bad example

IIPAUSEII

In silence think back over the tracks you have worked on in this book. Have there been any surprises or discoveries for you? Write them in this box.

Thank God for what he has taught you. If you want to you could share your discoveries with the group.

Meditation

Close your eyes, and have someone in the group read the Bible passage from John chapter 13. If possible read the whole passage from verse 1 to verse 14.

Imagine that you are one of the disciples at supper with Jesus. Picture him kneeling before you, taking off your shoes and washing your feet. What are you feeling? What do you say to Jesus? How does he reply?

Now imagine Jesus sitting beside you, saying: 'I have given you an example.' How will you follow his example?

How to use

This book has two aims....

■ **To help you hear what God has to say to you**
Of course there's no point in just hearing God speak for the sake of it. When God speaks to us he always wants us to change. So you need to decide how you will put what you hear into practice too.

■ **To help you grow together as a group**
The Christian life is for living together. That means getting to know each other, sharing ideas, encouraging each other and challenging each other to follow Jesus.

Here's how it works....

Each track in this book is divided into four sections :

LOAD This is the section to get you started. It's a chance for all the members of the group to share their ideas and experiences. Ask someone to read the scene-setter story aloud to the rest of the group. Then work through the questions that follow. You should work by yourselves, in pairs or all together as indicated by the symbols beside the questions. But try to work through the questions at the same pace so that no one gets left behind. Every member of your group is special. So make sure that everyone gets a chance to contribute.

PLAY The aim of this section is to find out what God has to say to you through his Word, the Bible.

You can either get together on this section or work individually. *Read through the Bible passages with a pencil in your hand. If anything strikes you as interesting, make a note of it in the book.* If there's anything you don't understand, or any questions you'd like answered, write them in too. We've pencilled in a few questions that occurred to us, but you can add your own.

When you've had a chance to work through the Bible passages and scribbled down your comments and questions, *get together with the rest of the group and talk through the questions you have raised, and the ones we thought of.* If there are too many questions to work through, choose the most important ones, or save some for another session. See if you can work out what God is saying through the Bible.

FAST FORWARD This is where the action starts. What are you going to do about the things that God is saying to you? Work through these questions as you did before. The *Fast forward* section always gives an opportunity for the members of the group to encourage and affirm one another, to share discoveries and to make plans.

What will you do? is a test of how much you have changed in the light of what you think God is saying. When it comes to the crunch what will you do? Decide for yourself then share your answer with the group. Be honest!

Tough talking is an optional section, mostly for older groups who like to struggle with hard questions. There are no easy answers here.

his book....

Going further is another optional section. It is not intended for you to use in the group session, but you may want to read through these passages in the week after the meeting to understand the subject even better. And they may help you with some of the *Tough talking* questions.

॥PAUSE॥ At the end of each track, take a *Pause* and spend some time focussing on God. Some groups will want to sing together or have a time of open prayer. If your group is not used to worship and praying together start with a few of the simpler ideas.

Making it work ...

Getting going

Every group meeting should start with a fun time to help everyone to relax together. This is particularly important if the members of the group don't know each other very well, or if there are new members. Ideas for breaking the ice are contained in the *Meeting points* section of the book. Pick on one or two of these ideas and enjoy them together. Don't be tempted to miss out this important warm-up stage of the group's meeting.

So much to do....so little time!

Different groups have different amounts of time available. Each track contains at least enough material for a whole evening together. Many groups won't be able to manage all the material at a single sitting. Don't worry! Either split the material over two or more sessions, or else select a couple of exercises from each section. It is much better to cover a few questions well than to try to do everything quickly. If one question seems particularly interesting or important for your group, spend longer on it. If there's a question that doesn't apply so much to you, just skip it.

Who's in charge?

Every group needs a leader. But it doesn't necessarily have to be the same person all the time. This book is designed so that group members could take it in turns to lead sessions. This is good experience, and it can also help to build the group if everyone agrees to co-operate with the session leader.

Here are some do's and don'ts for people leading a group session....

....do prepare!

Look through the material before the meeting. Decide what *Meeting points* you will use. Think about how long you want to spend on each section. Look carefully at the Bible passages and look up anything you think people may not understand. It may help if you have looked through the *Going further* passages too.

....don't panic!

The group leader doesn't have to know all the answers. If there are things that you don't know or questions that you can't answer, that's OK! It might be helpful to have a Bible commentary or handbook available so that you can check out any tricky questions. And you can always make a note to ask someone for help and report back to the group.

....do make sure everyone has a chance to contribute.
The leader will need to make sure that quieter people are able to join in the group discussions as well as more noisy ones. The leader will also make sure that it's not always the same people who are asked to share their answers or read out the stories.

....don't dominate!
The group belongs to everyone and everyone should be able to contribute. It's your job to make sure they can. Don't allow the group to be dominated by one person....especially if that person is yourself! If you are an adult leader of a teenage group you will need to be particularly careful to make sure that everyone is allowed to make their own discoveries and move at their own pace.

....do keep things moving.
It's your job to get the group together at the start of the session, and to decide how long to spend on each section. Gently make sure that everyone knows where the session is going. 'I think it's time we moved on now.' 'We'll have two minutes in pairs now, then we'll come together to discuss our answers.' 'Does anyone mind if we skip this next question?'

Notes for each track

Theme
The tracks in this book look at different aspects of power. The first track looks at God's overall plan for the world: to humble the powerful and lift up the powerless. This provides a context for the other tracks, when we think about the limited power of the Devil, and the ways that human beings use and abuse power. Explain this theme to the group before you begin the series.

Here are some notes to help you to plan for each group meeting.

Track 1
What is God's action plan?
This track is about the plan God has for the world. The Bible sometimes calls it the kingdom of God. In this track you will discover that the way things are done in the kingdom of God is totally different to the way things are done in the kingdoms of this world.

Load Some members of your group may have experience of bullying, so treat the subject with sensitivity. But try not to get too side-tracked from the main theme of the section, which is the experience of unfairness.

Play If your group is new to Serendipity you will need to explain how this section works. Make sure you have read the instructions in the 'How to use this book' section.

To many young people the claims of Jesus in the second paragraph and the instructions he gives in the final paragraph will seem ridiculous. Adults need to listen to the young people here to recapture the feeling of shock that Jesus' audience must have felt when he said these things.

Fast forward Skip the 'group' question if it is too complicated for your group, and concentrate on the one that follows it.

Where a question is marked with a 'solo' symbol you could simply ask, 'Would anyone *like* to share their answer?'

Pause Making wall-charts could take anything from ten minutes to an hour. Don't do it if you are very pushed for time.

Track 2
Can God beat the Devil?
This study is about the occult, and particularly about the power of Jesus to overcome the works of the Devil. If you are tempted to skip this session, think twice. Occult practices are more widespread amongst young people than we sometimes like to believe. Make sure that the power and the victory of Jesus comes over strongly in this session, as it does in the Bible passages. It might also be important to offer to talk privately with individuals who have had experiences of the occult. If you don't feel competent to do this, try to find somebody local who is.

Load Don't miss out the last question in this section.

Fast forward You must decide whether it will be appropriate for your group to engage in a discussion about their experiences of the occult. But do make sure that you focus on the first four questions about the power of Jesus.

Tough talking Some young Christians have very strong feelings on the subject of rock music. Bear in mind that a young person's choice of music is very closely bound up with their identity....so if the music is challenged, the young person can feel very threatened.

Track 3
Money and things : who's in charge?
This track is about money and possessions. Jesus taught that the way we handle money

and possesions was an indication of whether our priorities were right.

Load Remember that the aim of the *Load* section is to allow the group to express their own feelings and opinions and to 'tell it how they see it'. So don't allow the group to *criticise* each others' priorities at this stage.

Fast forward When you look at the group question, try to find specific practical suggestions for ways that the group members can help each other. Don't be content with vague ideas.

Pause Try to be imaginative in answering the first question. But then, once again, be practical and try to look for projects that you really could do.

Track 4
Power and prejudice : who wins?
This is a track looking at various sorts of prejudice. The Bible is very clear that all human beings are of equal value irrespective of their race, class, gender or anything else.

Load If you feel that your group could handle it, why not role-play the conversation between Angie and the head teacher. Divide into pairs and improvise their conversation, starting with the questions printed in the book. If it's going well, continue their conversation beyond the printed questions.

Fast forward When you have looked at the question about how the Pharisee could overcome his prejudice, you may want to relate it to your own situation and ask how you can best overcome prejudice.

The idea of telling group members what

is special about them may feel a bit strange at first. But if you can do it, you will find it makes people feel appreciated and valued.

Pause This exercise takes imagination and sensitivity. If you feel your group is not ready for it, you could simplify it a bit by keeping your eyes open and just asking "What would you do if Jesus was hungry?" and so on.

Track 5
Should we always do as we're told?
This track asks how Christians should treat people in authority. There are no easy answers when those in authority are sometimes opposed to God.

Load The 'finish the sentences' question is important. The Bible suggests that we should always obey people in authority when they are acting within their legitimate sphere of authority. So it's important to think about *why* the individuals in question have authority.

Fast forward The job-allocation exercise is partly for fun, and partly to help group members think imaginatively about each other's gifts and appreciate what is special about each other. Encourage group members to think why they are allocating particular jobs to particular people, but don't force them to share their reasons with the whole group.

Track 6
How should Christians handle power?
This track looks at the example Jesus set.

Play The question about Judas, (starting 'Does God sometimes take the bad things people do...?') is a difficult one. It should not be the first question you discuss together.

Fast forward There are no right or wrong answers to the question about the most important concerns for a follower of Jesus. Different Christians will have different priorities. Talk about why people have chosen the answers they have.

The key question in this track is the one about people you look up to and people who look up to you. Leave time to think about this. Some people may need your help to think of people who look up to or respect them.

Keep in touch with Serendipity

Serendipity is more than just a brand name for this book of group meetings. We exist to provide all sorts of help for those who work with young people or adults: Bible study outlines, resource evenings, training for leaders of small groups. If you would like us to keep you posted with news of future books and events, cut out this box and send it to us.

NAME ....

ADDRESS ....

....

....

I am particularly interested in:
  youth groups .... {tick as
  adult groups .... {appropriate

Send to: Serendipity UK, 48 Peterborough Road, London SW6 3EB